Christmas Elf Handbook

By Melissa Spencer

Christmas Elf Handbook is part of the full range of Elves and Elf Accessories at

www.merryelfmas.com

Christmas Elf Handbook

Since Buddy the Elf first came to visit us four years ago, Christmas time for our family has been transformed. We no longer spend weeks busily preparing just for one special day, before the sales start on Boxing Day and everything goes back to normal.

Buddy comes to stay on 1st December and we have 25 days of fantastic Christmas fun. It is a magical time of year and I am so happy to share our experiences with you, and help you begin this wonderful tradition for your own family. With this simple guide, you can bring some Elf magic into your home and create marvelous memories for your children.

After finding that affordable Elf goodies were hard to find, last year I set up Merry Elfmas to provide everything Elf Host Families need, and have an alternative to expensive branded items.

On the website www.merryelfmas.com, I have collected together all our favourite ideas, activities, printables, and links. I have also created a free downloadable Elf Kit, along with an online store so you can buy your Elf and activities to get you started.

And now, all the information you need is here in this book!

What are Magic Elves?

Santa's little helpers are sent to stay with specially selected children in the month leading up to Christmas, and bring with them some Christmas spirit and a sprinkling of Elf magic.

Elves come alive during the night and can get up to some cheeky antics, as well as bring fun activities and surprises. Children love waking up to find out what their Elf has been up to while no-one was looking.

Some Elves may simply hide in a different place each night, some may get up to a bit of mischief, and some may turn your house into a winter wonderland!

When Santa drops by on Christmas Eve, the Elves hitch a ride back to the North Pole until they visit again next year.

What do Elves do?

Often Elves are given the task of checking if children should be on Santa's naughty or nice list. Some Elves return to the North Pole each night to report back to Santa, and others can have report cards to fill in to let Santa know about children's acts of kindness or naughtiness. This can be a useful way of managing children's challenging behaviour, however we use the Elf Report to encourage and reward kindness.

Some of Buddy's activities help us to spread Christmas cheer and learn the joy of giving. For some families, their Elf visit has nothing to do with behaviour at all, it is simply about having lots of family fun.

Elf visits needn't cost a lot of money; antics often just involve items found around the home and a little imagination. Elves tend to need a bit of grown-up help during their visit, and later in the guide, there are lots of ideas for antics for each day of your Elf's stay.

To touch or not to touch?

Traditionally, Elves are not to be touched or else they lose their magic. But it really is up to you to choose.

Families have different rules for their Elf - some Elves can't be touched or they lose their magic, some hide each night, some get up to mischief, some leave little gifts. It all depends on what suits you and your family, and whether your Elf comes with its own instruction book that you wish to follow.

Some parents feel that having a no-touching rule keeps the magic alive and prevents the Elf from becoming just another toy. When accidental touching happens, Elf magic can be restored with the sprinkling of Elf Dust (glitter or cinnamon), or by temporarily sending the Elf back to the North Pole.

In some households, grown-ups can touch the Elf (so the Elf doesn't have to stay in the same mischievous place during the daytime), and some Elves can be touched by adults wearing gloves. But it really is up to you to choose. Our Elf, Buddy, is happy to be played with and loves cuddles with his best little human friend!

Being able to respectfully touch our Elf means his night time shenanigans can be cleared away in the mornings, and he can be moved out of harm's (ie. the dog's) way.

What do you need to start?

There are three essentials:

1. An Elf
2. Imagination
3. A sense of humour!

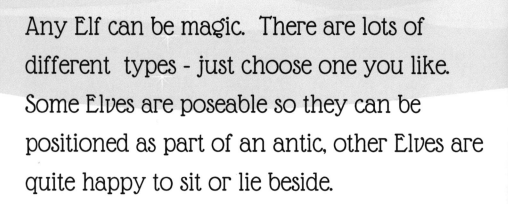

Any Elf can be magic. There are lots of different types - just choose one you like. Some Elves are poseable so they can be positioned as part of an antic, other Elves are quite happy to sit or lie beside.

A £30 Elf is no more magical than one that costs £1. Children will love their Elf for the things he does, not because he has the latest expensive imported aviator jacket.

To make the experience more magical, and to help get your family's new Elf tradition started, you can download a free Elf Kit from *www.merryelfmas.com*.

Get Your
FREE
Elf Kit
From
www.merryelfmas.com

The Elf Kit contains a letter from Santa, that explains some families are specially chosen to have an Elf come to stay. This can be sent to your children at the end of November to build their excitement and so they have time to understand what is happening.

There is also a letter to download for your Elf to introduce him/herself, along with a copy of an Elf Report they can fill in during their stay.

Elf Names

Your Elf will need a name.

If you need some suggestions, try this!

1ST LETTER OF YOUR FIRST NAME

A- Merry
B- Happy
C- Tiny
D- Cookie
E- Pixie
F- Jolly
G- Jingle

H- Elfie
I- Snowy
J- Tinsel
K- Bauble
L- Holly
M- Twinkie
N- Perky

O- Buddy
P- Trixie
Q- Elvis
R- Tinker
S- Bubbles
T- Glitz
U- Winx

V- Jinx
W- Noel
X- Rudy
Y- Belle
Z- Zippy

MONTH YOU WERE BORN

JAN- Pointy-Ears
FEB- Glitter-Balls
MAR- Pickle-Pants
APR- McJingles
MAY- Snickerdoodle
JUN- Sugarplum

JUL- Twinkle-Toes
AUG- McSprinkle
SEP- Candy-Cane
OCT- Jingleberry
NOV- Snowflake
DEC- Jolly-Jangles

December Planner 2015

Monday	Tuesday	Wednesday	Thursday	Friday	Saturday	Sunday
	1	2	3	4	5	6
7	8	9	10	11	12	13
14	15	16	17	18	19	20
21	22	23	24	25	Notes	

Also included in the free Elf Kit is an Elf Activity Planner for you to fill in with your antic plans.

Your Elf antics can be based around existing Christmas plans, for example, decorating the Christmas tree with pants, leaving a treasure hunt to find pantomime tickets, be found writing a Christmas wish list before a visit to see Santa, or be found trying to bake cookies for a school Christmas party.

Our Elf tends to do a mixture of mischief, leaving little treats and activities,and making plans for Christmas excursions. He very kindly puts up all the Christmas decorations and leaves craft kits to make little gifts for school friends, but sometimes also makes an extraordinary mess!

Your antics can be chosen bearing in mind the age and interests of your children, the items you have available, and things you might do ordinarily such as reading a Christmas story book. Antics can be as simple or elaborate as you like. Some of my son's favourite antics have been the cheap and easy ideas, like when Buddy hid inside a balloon. (Although one of my favourites was when Buddy arranged for us to visit a chocolate factory!).

You can make and buy accessories or 'props' too - your Elf may like an Elf Passport, a bed or sleeping bag, a pet reindeer, a journal, some magic snow - just think miniature and silly!

Your Elf's Arrival

1st December is the big day the Elves make their way from the North Pole to their host family's home, so you need to think about how your Elf will make his grand entrance.

Some children wake up to find their Elf has prepared a North Pole Breakfast and is waiting for them on the table. The North Pole Breakfast (NPB) is a Christmas breakfast feast, with Christmas tableware, decorations, and either Christmas-themed foods or the Elves' favourite, lots of sweet goodies.

We've had a few types of North Pole Breakfasts, my favourite being an Elf Movie-inspired plate of spaghetti covered with sweeties and syrup (not quite a culinary delight, but very funny!).

There are many ways for your Elf to arrive. So far, Buddy has been delivered in the post, arrived in a large Christmas sack on the back door step, appeared on the sofa, and come by hot air balloon.

Buddy usually arrives with an advent calendar, his bed and a letter. He has previously brought with him a photo album of all his favourite moments from the previous year, and last year, brought a beautiful memory blanket.

It has recently become popular for Elves to arrive through their own little Elf Door that had magically appeared on a skirting board a few days prior.

If this is all sounding like a lot of hard work, it really doesn't have to be. You can do as little or as much Elfing as you want to. You may discover, as so many Elf parents do, that grown-ups enjoy Elf magic just as much as the children!

I start planning for our Elf's visit months in advance because I love it! I love finding new Elf paraphernalia and collect ideas from Pinterest all year round.

I'm always delighted and inspired by this crazy Elf phenomenon and the creative ingenuity of some parents to ensure their little ones will have amazing childhood memories of Christmas. Hopefully our children will continue this lovely tradition with their own little ones in the future.

Saying goodbye

Both parents and children can feel a little sad when the time comes for their Elf to head back to the North Pole on Christmas Eve. Thankfully, the excitement of discovering Santa has visited and left some gifts, is a welcome distraction in the morning.

There is a farewell letter from your Elf to download in the free Elf Kit. It says how excited they are to get to travel in Santa's sleigh and to try not to feel sad, but remember the good times shared.

Our Elf leaves his letter along with a Christmas Eve Box in the afternoon. The box contains a few leaving gifts such as new pyjamas (perfect for Christmas morning photos), a Christmas story book for bedtime, and maybe a DVD, snowman soup (hot chocolate), some sweeties, and other little goodies I have come across.

Buddy also likes to leave a keepsake as a reminder of his visit. These have included a snowglobe with a photo of him with my son, an Elf photo frame, Buddy's little plush pet dog, and a baby reindeer.

When bedtime comes, we leave out some snacks for Santa and his reindeer with, Buddy snuggled up in his bed ready to be collected for his journey home.

Inquisitive minds

As children get a older, their curiosity can lead to them ask a few awkward questions. I am always equally as surprised, bemused and intrigued by Buddy's actions, and mostly put everything down to Elf Magic. If need be, your child could write a letter to their Elf asking their question, to allow some extra response thinking time.

WHY DOESN'T EVERY CHILD HAVE AN ELF TO STAY?

All families celebrate Christmas differentlyChildren all around the world are specially selected to receive an Elf visit. If your child has an Elf, they have been very lucky.

HOW DOES OUR ELF GET THROUGH SUCH A SMALL DOOR?

All part of the Elf Magic that enables them to come alive and travel back and forth to the North Pole through the door. But also Elves don't mind having to stoop to squeeze through small doors.

WHY CAN SOME ELVES BE TOUCHED AND OTHERS CAN'T?

All Elves are different, just like us. They come in all shapes and sizes, have different personalities, have different jobs to do in the North Pole, and some Elves even live in Woodland rather than with Santa. Likewise, some Elves can be held and some can have bedtime cuddles, whereas others can't be touched without losing their magic. Also, some parents make special requests to Santa to allow their Elf to be touched.

WHY IS THIS SHOP SELLING ELVES?

The Elves that are seen for sale in shops are not real – they are toy Elves that are sometimes given to the younger children who get so upset when their real Elf goes back to the North Pole. The toy Elves can also be bought for those children who aren't able to touch their real Elf. But if the toy Elves were sprinkled with magic Elf dust, who knows what may happen?!

WHY HASN'T OUR ELF MOVED?

Sometimes Elves don't move if they are very comfortable where they are or if they are coming down with a cold. Sometimes Elves don't move if they're disappointed with a child's behaviour or if they need a child to be extra kind to boost their Christmas spirit.

WHY IS OUR ELF IN YOUR WARDROBE/UNDER YOUR BED/IN THIS DRAWER?

On occasion, Elves pop in for a surprise at other times of the year, and like to hide somewhere children will find them.

Return Visits

It's up to each individual Elf to decide whether they will return for short visits during the year, whether they send birthday cards or postcards, or whether they are too busy making toys and will just come again in the run up to Christmas.

Buddy came to visit on Easter Sunday this year, which was a lovely surprise for my son, and I'm pretty sure he plans to join in with birthday celebrations too.

As my son will be 8, Buddy and I are making the most of the magic while it is still alive, before the dreaded day when he no longer... (can't bring myself to say the words!).

Some words of advice from a wise old Elf Mama

There is no right or wrong way to have an Elf come to stay - you can choose your own family traditions to suit you. The most important thing is you, your children and your Elf have lots of fun.

Place your Elf's bed under the Christmas tree - if he goes to bed with your child, he may not be able to slip out unnoticed during the night

Keep it simple - don't add stress to your Christmas preparations

You don't need to spend a fortune - many favourite antics are free

Don't cram too much in - save some ideas for next year!

 Your Elf crafts don't have to be perfect!

 Stay flexible - if you run out of time in the day, you don't have to stay up until 2am making intricate paper snowflakes! Swap, change and simplify antics as you need to

 Save a couple of really quick ideas for nights when you're tired

 Before you pack up all your Elfy bits and pieces after Christmas, make a note of any leftover accessories and ideas for next year

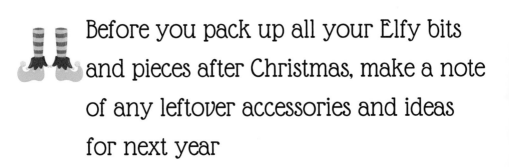

Next year

The following years your Elf comes to stay are still so exciting. Your children will remember all the fun they had before and will look forward to their little Elf friend coming to stay again. Your Elf will have much more of an idea of the kinds of mischief to get up to, and your family will have begun its own Elfing traditions.

Your Elf should come up with new antics each year to keep visits fresh and interesting. There are so many ideas on the Internet for inspiration, and you may want to repeat a few favourites, such as the North Pole Breakfast (maybe alternating with a North Pole Dinner), and the Christmas Eve Box. You can add some props when your Elf runs out of ideas around the house, and there are many free printables you can use.

Your child's interests change as they get older, which will present lots of new possibilities too. Buddy always ends up with far too many ideas for the number of days he's here, so although we're coming up to our 5th visit, we're still full of ideas.

MAKE MAGICAL MEMORIES

and have FUN!

24 Quick and Easy Antics

Elf found having
snowball fight
with other toys

Elf found on
computer
having created
Elf Yourself clip -
www.elfyourself.com

Elf leaves a
letter to Santa
writing kit

5

Elf daws
moustache on
children in the
night

Elf found
making cakes

6

7

Elf leaves Magic Elf seeds

8

Find gingerbread man or candy canes
with elf covered in crumbs

Elf found trapped inside balloon

Elf found playing games with other toys

11

Elf leaves little gift eg.
a Christmas lolly or book

Elf writes message in spray snow,
shaving foam or sweets

12

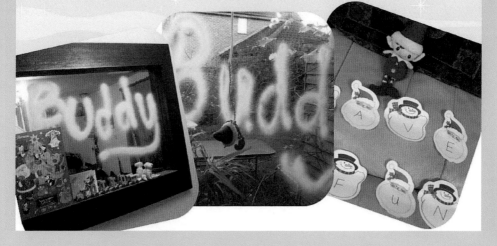

Elf puts up the Christmas Decorations or is found tangled in decorations

Elf decorates Christmas tree with children's pants

15 Elf found reading to other toys

Elf found making paper snowflakes **16**

Elf leaves Christmas crafts kit
(or Easter if you buy
the wrong thing!)

Elf hides candy canes or chocs

Elf Leaves note
saying check email
(PNP message rom Santa)
www.portablenorthpole.com

Elf Treasure Hunt or
Elf plays 'Pin the Nose to the Snowman'

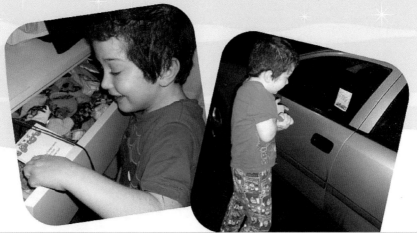

Elf leaves note about visit to see
Santa or trip to the cinema

21

22

Elf covers bathroom with
toilet roll and makes a
snowman toilet roll

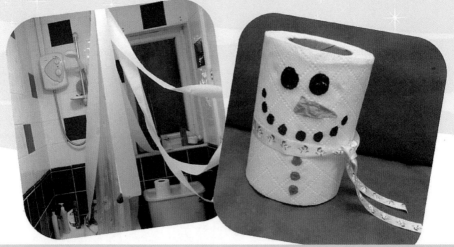

Elf leaves Christmas colouring or activity book

23

24

Elf hosts North Pole Breakfast

Elf leaves Christmas Eve Box plus
goodbye letter, before heading
back to the North Pole

24

Some Favourites

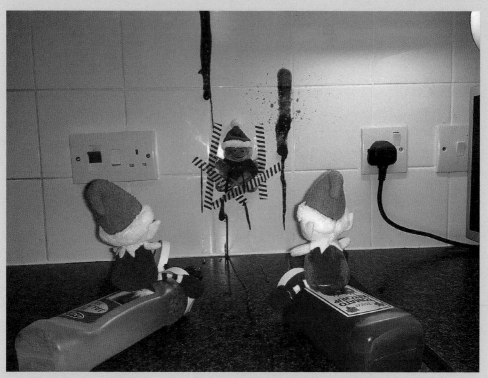

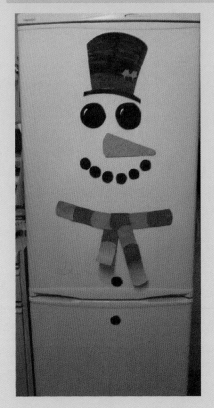

WORST COOKIES EVER! Do NOT leave for Santa!

Merry Elfmas!